The Little Book of
SUCCESS

The Little Book of Success

Copyright © 2019 Kevin Kearney.

All rights reserved. Printed in the United States of America. No part of this book may be used or reproduced without the express permission of the author, except in the case of brief quotations in critical articles and reviews.

For information, address Kevin Kearney:
kckearn@yahoo.com

ISBN: 978-0-578-51972-2   U.S.A.

Published by Big Heart Books, Mill Valley, CA

Illustrations by Dobrodzei, Shutterstock
Cover and book design: Gilman Design, Larkspur, CA

Dedication

For the dreamers and young entrepreneurs.
The world needs you to be a leader,
but you need to start with yourself.
May you move forward with a brave heart.

The Little Book of
SUCCESS

KEVIN KEARNEY

Introduction

In all honesty, I wrote this book for myself. Like most people, I was born with a few challenges. Early on, the biggest were that I was very tall for my age, I had a September birthday, and I had undiagnosed learning differences—problems with learning to read, spatial/relational challenges and sequential memory. Starting in kindergarten, I was moved from grade to grade because I had been "too tall" to be in the previous grade, even though I was clearly not keeping up with my classmates. I ended up failing and repeating second grade and went to summer school just to be ready to keep up. These experiences gave me a profound appreciation for putting things in an order that was easier for my mind to understand and remember.

As I got older, I would pick up management, leadership and personal growth books to improve myself and stay competitive. As I read the books, I found that even books that appeared simple—i.e. *Seven Habits of Highly Effective People*—contained a lot of information and could quickly become overwhelming.

The most difficult time in my life was the transition from high school to college, then into the workforce. Truly, it is a difficult time for most people struggling with what to do for the rest of their lives while still making a paycheck for today. This book is for those people in transition, looking for straight-forward tips and advice on how to be more successful. I have done my best to distill some of the best ideas and concepts. I have also included a list of my favorite books and resources at the back of this book. There is no shortcut—it is hard work, but these nuggets of wisdom in an easily referenced book would have meant the world to me.

I have profound appreciation and gratitude to the coaches, mentors, and resources I have partnered with along the way. My partial list would include: Zig Ziglar, Les Brown, Brian Buffini, Lorna Hines, Coaches Training Institute (CTI), and the list goes on.

My goal is that you will start your own Personal Success Journal, documenting your progress on the journey. My hope is that it will transform your life in some way.

– Kevin Kearney

Personal Matters

It's not just a dream
when you decide
to make it your life!

You Matter

By the time you are reading this, you have probably been beaten down and pressured by friends, family and society to fit the mold they have for you. This life requires you to lead your own life. I would encourage you to throw out all that undue influence and **BE YOURSELF**. The more we try to hide ourselves or be who others want us to be, the more we create anxiety within ourselves.

This book is about living your life on purpose. Not many of us know what we want to do when we grow up, even when we are grown up. Start to ask yourself questions: What is important to you? What difference do you want to make in your world or the world? What do you need to start doing or STOP doing in order to be yourself and just do it? Once you have a little direction, *the road will present itself.*

I like the tree as a metaphor for life. The roots are your internal self and the trunk, limbs and leaves are your external self. The upper part is susceptible to being blown around and broken yet grows stronger over time and exposure. The roots must be as big and deep as the tree is tall for it to keep its strength.

Success is about working on your inner self so that your outer self can grow to its potential.

Only you know your deepest dreams and desires. These change from time to time and it is a lifelong process of discovery. The world needs you to be you and you need you to be you. Be good to yourself—and to others. We are all on our own journeys.

You must learn and grow to reach your full potential.

Defining Success

Google defines **success** as:
"suc·cess – noun -   /suk-ses/

1. The accomplishment of an aim or purpose.
– "the president had some success in restoring confidence"

2. The attainment of popularity or profit.
– "the success of his play"

3. A person or thing that achieves desired aims or attains prosperity.
– "I must make a success of my business."

4. The outcome of an undertaking, specified as achieving or failing to achieve its aims.
– "the good or ill success of their maritime enterprises"

It is important to remember that only you can define what success looks like for you. Do not judge yourself by others' goals, aspirations, and achievements. You alone are responsible for your happiness. You alone set your standard. Set big goals and let your daily actions do the rest.

A person has the ability to change their future by making a conscious decision today.

In the Middle

Let's start with some perspective. It is important to know where we fit in.

1. There is a 99.9% chance that there is someone in the world who is better, smarter and richer than you.

2. There is a 99.9% chance that there is someone in the world who is not as good, not as smart and does not have as much money as you.

Get used to being somewhere in the middle and being happy—AND, be aware that you are capable of so much more.

By the way, not everyone will like you, either. Get used to that fact. It will help you to understand that in a world of 7 billion people, there will be enough people that do like you to make you phenomenally successful.

A little perspective in life can make challenges more surmountable.

Say What?

Let's start with you.

What do you say to yourself when no one else is around? Who is your inner critic? What have people said to you that takes you out of your power? What negative thoughts, ideas or stories do you have that keep you from being your best self? Limiting Beliefs? Take note! You have the power to change or reprogram these thoughts. Make a list of affirmations to keep in your journal, on your wall or in your wallet. You can read these frequently to remind yourself of who you are and what you want to accomplish.

An Affirmation *is a statement about who you are or want to be in the present tense.*

Some examples would be: "I am smart. I am funny. I am a good person and people like me." Two of my favorites are: "I did it before, and I can do it again!" and "If they can do it, I can do it!"

Write a few affirmations for yourself on the next page:

> *"Whatever your mind can conceive and believe, it can achieve."*
>
> – Napoleon Hill

Fear of Failure

So many people are afraid of failure. Don't be! Failure is inevitable but you have a choice. To accept failure is to learn and to grow. Rita Mae Brown said that "good judgment comes from experience and experience comes from bad judgment". If you are not experiencing "NOs" or failures, you cannot gain the experience you need to get to the "YESs" and ultimate success.

Go out and fail. Big.

I recommend taking a class in improvisation or joining a Toastmasters group. It will give you confidence in speaking your thoughts, allow you to fail safely, to think on your feet and keep moving.

False	**F**orgetting	**F**orget
Evidence	**E**very	**E**verything
Appearing	**A**vailable	**A**nd
Real	**R**esource	**R**un

What are your biggest FEARS? What resources do you need to overcome them?

"Success is not final, failure is not fatal; it is the courage to continue that counts."

– Winston Churchill

Live Each Day to the Fullest

I am not a religious person but I am spiritual. I came across this poem by S.H. Payer after college and it made an impact on me. The lines about being your best self and making decisions the best you can particularly. I hope you like it.

Live each day to the fullest.

Get the most from each hour, each day, and each age of your life.

Then you can look forward with confidence, and back without regrets.

Be yourself but be your best self.

Dare to be different and follow your own star.

Don't be afraid to be happy and enjoy what is beautiful.

Love with all your heart and soul. Believe that those you love, love you.

When you are faced with decision, make that decision as wisely as possible, then forget it.

The moment of absolute certainty never arrives.

Above all, remember that God helps those who help themselves.

Act as if everything depended on you and pray as if everything depended on God.

– S. H. Payer

Optimism and Enthusiasm

For some people, optimism is not a natural state. Life is hard and things will come up that discourage you. I am not saying you must be happy all the time, because you won't. More often than not, you need to find your enthusiasm. According to Zig Ziglar, the IASM at the end of the word enthusIASM stands for "I Am Sold Myself!" Go back to the affirmations and add "I am enthusiastic!"

What are you optimistic and enthusiastic about? How can you leverage these things?

"One of the things I learned the hard way was that it doesn't pay to get discouraged. Keeping busy and making optimism a way of life can restore your faith in yourself."
– Lucille Ball

Confidence

People respond positively to confidence. Life is like a play where everyone knows their part. You must know what you are trying to accomplish, who the key players are to help get you there and know your part. Industry dialogs or elevator pitches can help you increase your business. Find or create them, memorize them and then find a partner to practice, practice, practice.

The better you know your part, the more confident you can be.

What areas of your life are you confident in? How can you leverage these skills?

_____
_____
_____
_____
_____
_____
_____
_____
_____

"Believe in yourself! Have faith in your abilities! Without a humble but reasonable confidence in your own powers, you cannot be successful or happy."
— Norman Vincent Peale

Give Back

My life seems more fulfilling and I have a better perspective when I am volunteering to help others. I urge you to get involved with an organization that you are passionate about—more than one if you have time and opportunity.

Give of your time until you can afford to give money.

For me, these experiences had many benefits besides the smiles on the faces of those we helped. They also taught me skills: working with other people, being dependable, being punctual, and with some experience, I was able to learn leadership skills as well.

What are some organizations you believe in that you could become involved with?

_____

_____

_____

_____

_____

_____

> "I believe in one thing – that only a life lived for others is the life worth living."
>
> – Albert Einstein

Growth Matters

Impossible?
I'm Possible!

Personal growth is simple,
but it is not easy.

Incremental Improvement

Small changes over time can produce big results! You may have heard someone say, "focus on your strengths; forget your weaknesses." I agree but also believe there are ways to improve your strengths AND your weaknesses. You can read books and take classes that will help you be a better you. Always be learning. Make it a lifelong journey. Always remember that you can partner with or hire people for whom your weaknesses are strengths. Do not let your weaknesses hold you back! Always do your best. It will get better every day.

What are your strengths? What are your weaknesses?
It is sometimes helpful to ask some close friends or family members about this one.

_____
_____
_____

_____
_____
_____

_____
_____
_____

All our life experiences prepare us for the next great adventure.

The following poem is another one of my favorites. It reminds me to give back to the community and use my time wisely to help others.

A Splendid Torch

I am of the opinion that my life belongs to
the whole community and as long as I live,
it is my privilege to do for it whatsoever I can.
I want to be thoroughly used up when I die,
for the harder I work, the more I live.
I rejoice in life for its own sake.
Life is no "brief candle" for me.
It is a sort of splendid torch which I
have got hold of for a moment
and I want to make it burn as brightly
as possible before handing it on
to the future generations.

– George Bernard Shaw

Personal Team

To be effective in this life, you must have advocates. Ask yourself who are your teammates. Are they moving you forward or holding you back? You must become your own coach, then have mentors and people you admire to model yourself after. A mentor can speed up your progress, so choose someone who inspires you and is willing to help you. Brian Buffini says: "before you step out of your comfort zone, step into someone else's."

Another great way to expand your network and be around like-minded people is to form a mastermind. A mastermind is a group of people who inspire each other to do more. The people who hold you back should not be on your team. To be successful, recruit people who support you and move you forward.

Who is on your support team? With whom should you spend less time?

_____

_____

_____

_____

_____

_____

"If you want to go fast, go alone. If you want to go far, go together."

– African Proverb

Balance

Enjoy the process! So many people (including me) spend so much time trying to achieve their goals that they forget to stop and enjoy the journey. My friend Joe always tells me that people spend their youth trying to make money and then later in life spend their money to get back their youth! Find a way to integrate the two. Exercise, hike, bike, run, meditate, practice yoga…

What do you like to do that can provide balance in your life?

_____
_____
_____

_____
_____
_____

_____
_____
_____

_____
_____
_____

Living a balanced life is the only way to truly live.

Focus on the Outcome

There are many books and leaders that talk about written goals. It is also important to visualize your desired outcome – no matter how ridiculous or unreachable you believe it to be. I have found that the more goals you write down, the more you will start moving towards them—even if they are not your current focus. Just putting them down on paper starts to move you towards them. Ask yourself: How good can you stand it?

To achieve your objective—you must aim higher. Viktor Frankl gave a talk that is available on YouTube about setting goals. He likened the process to piloting an airplane to a destination. Because of the wind speed, direction and gravitational pull, you must adjust constantly in order to get where you are going. Think BIG! You will be happier with the results in the end.

"Even if you know where you are going, you will get run over if you just sit there!"

– Will Rogers

Goals and Stretch Goals

Take a minute to list a few goals on these next pages. These will change over time, so do not worry about having them just right.

What are your stretch goals? What would you do if there were no limits?

_____
_____
_____
_____
_____
_____
_____
_____
_____
_____
_____
_____
_____
_____
_____

Goals and Stretch Goals, cont.

Business Matters

Responsibility
Response-Ability

Your ability to respond and choose
your response is where the power comes
to take control of your future.

Abundance Mentality

This is one of the most important personal leadership and success ideas we will discuss. It is a big world out there AND there is enough out there for everyone. You just have to go get your share. If you embrace this idea, it will help you achieve what you define as success.
My coach Lorna Hines defines it below as the *Law of Abundance*:

Law of Abundance

1. *I have the ability to live a self-determined and accountable life that will create endless opportunity for my success. As a result, the fear of loss is not a threat to my wellbeing.*

2. *Abundance is limited only by my inability to use my time effectively.*

– Lorna Hines

Personal Accountability

Following the Law of Abundance, this is the next most important concept.

Law of Accountability

1. I have the responsibility for my own actions, failures, and success. The quality of my life will depend on my ability to be self-determined and accountable for the circumstances over which I can have control.

2. I cannot and should not become accountable for circumstances that are another's responsibility. If I shift accountability from where it belongs, I will limit my own and other's success.

– Lorna Hines

This is a poem by Edgar A. Guest that speaks to me. To the best of my ability, I have chosen to live my life as a builder. What would you choose?

A Builder or a Wrecker

*I watched them tear a building down
A gang of men in a busy town*

*With a ho-heave-ho, and a lusty yell
They swung a beam and the side wall fell*

*I asked the foreman, "Are these men skilled,
And the men you'd hire if you wanted to build?"*

*He gave a laugh and said, "No, indeed,
Just common labor is all I need."*

*"I can wreck in a day or two
What builders have taken a year to do."*

*And I thought to myself as I went my way
Which of these roles have I tried to play?*

*Am I a builder who works with care,
Measuring life by rule and square?*

*Am I shaping my work to a well-made plan
Patiently doing the best I can?*

*Or am I a wrecker who walks to town
Content with the labor of tearing down?*

– Edgar A. Guest

Time Management

The Pareto Principle states that 80% of outcome comes from 20% of the effort. It makes sense that you should pay attention to what actions you are doing that are achieving 80% of your results and focus on those items. What actions are you doing daily that are moving you forward? Lean into them.

Ever notice how much more effective you are just prior to a vacation? Here is a challenge for you: Live your life as if you are going on vacation next week.

What strategies do you employ to make you more productive in those few days?

_____
_____
_____
_____
_____
_____
_____
_____
_____

The best way to be productive is to focus on the things you do that give you the biggest results.

Being a Salesperson

If you were born on this planet and can read these lines, your life is determined by your ability to sell yourself. Many people do not like the idea of being in sales. If you think about it, you sell yourself to your boss, you sell yourself to your friends and family—you even sell yourself to—YOU!

Become good at sales. Sell with sincerity. You do not have to be someone you are not! To sell, you must also be comfortable with rejection and frustration. They are a part of the sales process.

What skills do you need to develop to become good at sales?

"When you show a man what he wants, he'll move heaven and earth to get it."

– Frank Bettger

Self-Employed

I encourage you to think of yourself as self-employed. You may need to have a job, but consider for many, job security is a thing of the past. It is your job to take care of you (and your family). This means you need to keep yourself employable throughout your career. Something could happen to your job or to you and you may no longer be able to do the same thing.

What are things you can do or study to keep yourself employable?

Taking the perspective that you are self-employed will help you keep yourself employable.

Grow Your Network

We all know people who can help us grow our business. The list may be short at first, but we add to that list as we meet new people.

There are many ways to grow your network. My favorites include local Chamber of Commerce mixers, Meetup groups, or other activities you enjoy that get you out meeting people. You can also expand your network by giving back to the community at your favorite non-profit. Some even travel to network!

Ivan Misner, the founder of Business Networking International (BNI), refers to having a "Givers Gain" mentality when it comes to your network. The idea is to give others referrals or connect them to someone who would be a great referral partner for them so that they want to refer business back to you. I could not agree more.

Who are the most influential people in your current network? Who do you need to meet to strengthen your connections? Who can you connect and make a beneficial relationship?

_____

_____

_____

> *"You can have everything you want in life if you just help enough other people get what they want!"*
>
> – Zig Ziglar

"YOU" Matters

The rest of your life starts today!

Next Chapter

The rest is yet unwritten and failure is inevitable! This is what makes life exciting. Quit trying to do what everyone else is doing. The most important thing is for you to figure it out—your way! Remember, there is no such thing as an overnight success.

It is hard work. I have had many failures and setbacks along the way. **The key to success is never giving up!** On the cover is a depiction of a person on a mountaintop planting a flag. It is time to look at your life and decide what your flag should represent. The following pages contain exercises to help solidify the ideas you have learned here. I wish you the best on your journey!

"I was looking for the key for years. But the door was always open."

– Aravind Adiga

Tell Your Story

Your first exercise is to tell your story. It is important to understand where you have been to get a clearer picture of where you are going. The better you can articulate this, the better you can see patterns and identify your values that will help you for the next exercises. This should include all the highlights AND struggles of your life so far. You will want another journal for this, but I am including some space to jot down your ideas and memories.

"Owning our story and loving ourselves through that process is the bravest thing that we will ever do."

– Brene Brown

Mission Statement

Now that we have gone through the previous exercises, it is time to get specific. First, the Mission Statement: your mission statement should include **who you are, what you stand for and why you do what you do.** It should be a framework for how you live your life. It should also inspire you and with reflection, should help you make difficult life choices.

To illustrate, I have included below my mission statement of 20 years. It has served me well and still inspires me.

In my life there are four areas that are important to me; me, my family, my career, and my community. However, the most important thing to remember to bring them all together is BALANCE!

My first commitment is to me. I regularly exercise, read, pray and meditate for my mental and spiritual development. I live a life of honesty, integrity, and character.

My second commitment is to my family. To love, honor, serve and have fun with my family. In addition, I will continue to develop my personal relationships with my family and friends.

My third commitment is to my business development. I work for myself and maintain a balanced budget that includes a healthy savings plan—I continue to develop my network and provide excellent customer service to my valued clients.

My final commitment is to my community. I regularly volunteer for community development projects and work with children.

You can tell by the writing that I am a straight-forward kind of guy. Your mission statement can also be fun and funny. A paragraph is enough. Start with your big ideas and gradually condense them to something short and sweet.

"If we did all we were capable of, we would literally astound ourselves."

– Thomas Edison

Write your personal mission statement below:

Life Purpose Statement

I have found that what made the most difference for me was when I took a class at Co-Active Training Institute (CTI) and wrote a life purpose statement. What is your life purpose? What is important to you? What impact do you want to have on the world? Take the time to dig deep and find what truly matters to you. Then write a statement you can own that will remind you of your purpose: a descriptive statement, for yourself alone, of what you do in the world and how you do it. It should be no more than a sentence, but you will glow with purpose when you have it.

Here is my current one:

I inspire personal leadership, with heart.

It fuels action for me.

I have provided some blank note pages to brainstorm and work on your ideas before you write yours.

_____
_____
_____
_____
_____
_____

Having a life purpose statement is the most powerful motivator to make your impact in the world.

Success Journal

Create your own "Personal Success Journal" documenting your Mission Statement, goals, favorite quotes and evidence of your success! In this, I would also include a page each year with a brief paragraph about how the year went. Make two columns—one for successes and the other for challenges—and finish it off with goals for next year. Below, write down your ideas and the headings you want in it. This should be a separate document or binder that you can add to over time. Have fun with it—create a cover, make it yours.

_____
_____
_____

_____
_____
_____

_____
_____
_____

_____
_____
_____

This is a poem I like to read each New Year's Eve.
It reminds me to think of what I accomplished last year
and what I want to accomplish for the next.

Victory

You are the man who used to boast
That you'd achieve the uttermost,
Someday
You merely wished to show,
To demonstrate how much you know
And prove the distance you can go…
Another year we've just passed through
What new ideas came to you?
How many big things did you do?
Time left twelve fresh months in your care
How many of them did you share
With opportunity and dare
Again, where you so often missed?
We do not find you on the list of makers good
Explain that fact!
Ah no, 'twas not the chance you lacked!
As usual, you failed to act.

– Herbert Kaufman

Recommended Reading

I recommend a wide range of books — from self-help to business and everywhere in between. They have all been important on my journey.

See You at the Top – Zig Ziglar

The Success Principles – Jack Canfield

What to Say When You Talk To Yourself – Chad Helmstetter, Ph.D

Awaken the Giant Within – Anthony Robbins

7 Habits of Highly Effective People – Stephen Covey

Outliers – Malcolm Gladwell

Compound Effect – Darren Hardy

Getting Things Done – David Allen

The Four Agreements – Don Miguel Ruiz

Think and Grow Rich – Napoleon Hill

The Science of Getting Rich – Wallace D. Wattles

You(2) – Price Pritchett, PH.D.

Taking Care of Business – Brian Buffini and Joe Niego

The Emigrant Edge – Brian Buffini

Good to Great – Jim Collins

29% Solution – Ivan Misner

Tribes – Seth Godin

Co-Active Leadership – Karen and Henry Kimsey-House

How I Raised Myself from Failure to Success in Selling – Frank Bettger

The Millionaire Next Door – Thomas J. Stanley

Trainings in Compassion – Norman Fischer

Awakening the Buddha Within – Lama Surya Das

A Path With Heart – Jack Kornfield

Positive Intelligence – Shirzad Chamine

Presence – Amy Cuddy

The Gifts of Imperfection – Brene Brown

The War of Art – Steven Pressfield

Subscribe to *DarrenDaily.com/Updates*

www.ingramcontent.com/pod-product-compliance
Lightning Source LLC
Chambersburg PA
CBHW062028290426
44108CB00025B/2827